Walking in Power

30 Days of Inspiration Devotional

Nichol Collins

Day 1- The Power of Prayer

"Do not be anxious about anything, but in everything, by prayer and petition, with thanksgiving, present your requests to God." ~Philippians 4:6

Anxiety can overwhelm, but this verse reminds us to let go of fear. Nothing is too insignificant for the Lord's attention. Instead of carrying the burden ourselves, we're encouraged to leave it on the altar, trusting Him to work in His wisdom and timing.

Satan's primary goal is to keep us distracted from prayer because we cancel his diabolical plans. When we connect with God through prayer, strongholds are broken, and Satan's schemes are exposed. Prayer is more than an activity—it's a lifestyle of intimacy with God. By developing a consistent prayer life, we invite Him to

Walking in Power

restore our joy. His presence fills us with peace, providing the strength to endure and the insight to navigate life's challenges.

The keys to unlocking wisdom and wealth in the Kingdom of God are found through prayer, worship, and decrees. Prayer aligns our hearts with God's will, worship invites His presence, and decrees release the power of heaven on earth.

"But the Lord is in His holy temple; let all the earth be silent before Him."
~Habakkuk 2:20

God is reigning in His holy temple, fully in control, and worthy of reverence. The call for the earth to be silent emphasizes awe, humility, and submission before His greatness. It's a moment to recognize His authority and trust in His divine plan.

Let us make prayer our priority today. In the quiet moments, we will find peace, direction, and the power to overcome any obstacle Satan tries to place in our path.

Nichol Collins

Day 2- A.C.T.S. of Prayer

"But the Lord is near to all who call on Him, to all who call on Him in truth." ~Psalm 145:18

The Lord is near and responsive to anyone who prays to Him with a genuine and honest heart. An article I came across on the internet introduced me to the basic forms of prayer, summarized as A.C.T.S.—Adoration, Contrition, Thanksgiving, and Supplication. Each of these elements helps draw us closer to God and align our hearts with His will.

Adoration is the foundation, where we express love, respect, and devotion to God, exalting Him for who He is. Contrition follows, as we acknowledge our shortcomings, repent, and seek forgiveness. Thanksgiving is the outpouring of gratitude for God's blessings, shifting our focus from our needs to His goodness. Supplication is when we humbly bring our requests to God, trusting He will answer according to His will.

As we nurture our prayer life, we must be intentional, resisting the temptation to engage in other activities that do not edify our spirit-man.

"Enter His gates with thanksgiving and His courts with praise; give thanks to Him and praise His name." ~Psalm 100:4

In biblical times, the temple gates were the entry point to the presence of God. Thanksgiving is our spiritual "entry pass" into His presence. It reflects an attitude of gratitude for His blessings, goodness, and faithfulness. "And His courts with praise" emphasizes that our worship should include both thanksgiving (for what God has done) and praise (for who He is).

Take a moment today to worship with a heart full of gratitude and reverence—encounter His presence and honor His holy name.

Day 3- God's Unwavering Word

"For the word of the Lord is right and true; he is faithful in all he does." ~Psalm 33:4

This verse reminds believers that God's words and actions are always right and reliable—He fulfills His promises without fail. In life, it's easy to be swayed by our circumstances—whether it's financial struggles, health issues, or emotional challenges. We must remember that our reality is not defined by what we see around us.

Do Not Allow Your Circumstance to Dictate What God Said!!

When things don't look the way we expect, it's crucial to hold on to what God has already revealed. His promises are not conditional on our present situation. He is faithful to fulfill every word He has spoken, even when the journey seems uncertain. Don't let fear, doubt, or frustration dictate your faith. Stand firm in God's promises, knowing that He is working behind the scenes.

Let your heart be anchored in His Word. Declare His truth over your life and trust that He will bring it to pass. Your circumstances may change, but the Word of God remains unshakable. Stand on His promises, and let them guide you through every season.

"Heaven and earth will pass away, but my words will never pass away."
~Matthew 24:35

Find solace in the fact that, while the world and everything in it will eventually fade, God's words are eternal and unchanging. His truth stands forever.

Day 4- Power Through the Spirit

"But ye shall receive power, after that the Holy Ghost is come upon you: and ye shall be my witnesses..." ~ Acts 1:8 (KJV)

Jesus, in His final moments with His disciples, made an incredible promise: they would be baptized with the Holy Ghost, receiving power to be His witnesses to the ends of the earth. This was a divine mandate for believers to experience the fullness of God's presence and power in their lives. The baptism of the Holy Spirit was not just about speaking in tongues or receiving gifts; it was about being empowered to live out the Gospel and share it boldly.

Jesus made it clear that the Holy Spirit's coming would transform them. He would provide the courage, enlightenment, and strength needed to carry out the mission set before them. This power would

Walking in Power

extend beyond their personal lives to influence the world around them, turning ordinary people into powerful witnesses of Christ's life-changing work.

As believers today, this same promise is available to us. Are you walking in the power of the Holy Spirit? Are you letting Him lead, guide, and empower you to fulfill God's purpose for your life?

"So if you sinful people know how to give good gifts to your children, how much more will your heavenly Father give the Holy Spirit to those who ask him."
~Luke 11:13 (NLT)

Day 5- The Evidence

"And they were all filled with the Holy Ghost, and began to speak with other tongues, as the Spirit gave them utterance." ~Acts 2:4

"And it shall come to pass in the last days, saith God, I will pour out of my Spirit upon all flesh: and your sons and your daughters shall prophesy, and your young men shall see visions, and your old men shall dream dreams." ~Acts 2:17

The outpouring of the Holy Spirit at Pentecost was a powerful moment that forever changed the course of humanity. In Acts 2:4, the disciples were filled with the Holy Ghost and began to speak in other tongues, marking the beginning of a new era where the Spirit of God would dwell within believers, equipping them to fulfill the Great Commission.

Walking in Power

Acts 2:17 reminds us that this promise extends beyond the first-century church to all generations. God's Spirit is poured out on all flesh, breaking barriers of age, gender, and status. This outpouring empowers us to prophesy, see visions, and dream dreams, aligning our hearts with the sacred will and purpose of God.

The same Spirit that filled the early believers is at work today, enabling us to speak God's truth, fulfill His mission, and experience His presence in profound ways. Let us embrace the power of the Holy Spirit and walk boldly in the gifts and callings He has placed on our lives.

Be encouraged—a winner cannot lose with power!

Day 6- Speaking Divine Mysteries

When we speak in tongues, we communicate directly with God, sharing mysteries and heavenly secrets that surpass human understanding. This unique form of exchange is encoded by the Holy Spirit, creating a language that even Satan cannot decipher.

Paul describes this beautifully:
"For if you have the ability to speak in tongues, you will be talking only to God, since people won't be able to understand you. You will be speaking by the power of the Spirit, but it will all be mysterious."
~1 Corinthians 14:2 (NLT)

This verse highlights the closeness and depth of connection that speaking in tongues brings. It is a powerful way to build yourself up in the Spirit, aligning your heart and mind with God's will. As you engage in this heavenly language, you unlock a supernatural dimension of worship, intercession, and revelation.

Remember, tongues is not meant to glorify ourselves but to deepen our relationship with God. It allows the Spirit to pray through us when words fail and to strengthen our faith as we walk in His purpose. Through this gift, we gain access to the hidden foresight and mysteries of heaven, empowering us to stand firm in spiritual warfare.

Day 7- The Highest Agreement

Speaking in tongues represents the highest form of the prayer of agreement. When we engage in this Spirit-led expression, we align our hearts and minds with God's perfect will, trusting that the Holy Spirit intercedes on our behalf. This spiritual partnership ensures that our prayers are in complete harmony with heaven, even when we are unsure how to pray.

Praying in tongues transcends our natural understanding, allowing the Spirit to communicate directly with God. It is a powerful reminder that our petitions are heard and that we can have confidence in His promises.

When we pray in tongues, we are not praying alone; the Holy Spirit is agreeing with us and interceding for us in ways we cannot comprehend. This covenant

Walking in Power

amplifies our prayers, ensuring they are aligned with God's will and perfectly tailored to our needs and His purpose.

Embrace the gift of tongues as a supernatural tool to deepen your intimacy with God and to experience the unparalleled power of the prayer of agreement.

The Apostle John reassures us of God's attentiveness to our prayers, telling us that if we know God hears us, we can be confident He will answer according to His will. *'And if we know that he hears us in whatever we ask, we know that we have the requests that we have asked of him.'* ~1 John 5:15 (ESV)

Day 8- Strengthened in the Spirit

Just as consistent workouts build physical stamina and muscle, your prayer language builds spiritual endurance and resilience. Praying in tongues is a celestial exercise that strengthens your inner man with might, keeping you spiritually fit and prepared for the battles of life.

The Apostle Jude emphasized the transformative power of this practice:
"But ye, beloved, building up yourselves on your most holy faith, praying in the Holy Ghost." ~Jude 20 (KJV)

Through praying in the Spirit, we expand our capacity to walk in greater levels of anointing and access spiritual realms beyond natural comprehension. This practice enhances our faith, and equips us to overcome challenges with strength and clarity.

Walking in Power

By incorporating tongues into your spiritual routine, you are fortifying your spirit, sharpening your discernment, and receiving heavenly strategies for your life. Embrace this gift as an essential part of staying spiritually fit and thriving in your walk with the Lord.

Day 9- Gateway to Gifts

"Now concerning spiritual gifts, brethren, I do not want you to be ignorant: ...for to one is given the word of wisdom through the Spirit, to another the word of knowledge through the same Spirit, to another faith by the same Spirit, to another gifts of healings by the same Spirit, to another the working of miracles, to another prophecy, to another discerning of spirits, to another different kinds of tongues, to another the interpretation of tongues. But one and the same Spirit works all these things, distributing to each one individually as He wills." ~1 Corinthians 12:1, 8-11

The gifts of the Spirit serve as manifestations of God's power and perception, functioning through those who are open and yielded to His Spirit. Speaking in tongues acts as a gateway to these gifts. As believers pray in tongues, they fuel their Spirit, creating an environment where other spiritual gifts can flow more freely. For instance, tongues can lead to interpretations that edify the church, or it may enhance discernment and understanding in prayer, paving the way for the word of wisdom, prophecy, or the working of miracles.

The Apostle Paul reminds us that these gifts are distributed by the Spirit as He wills. It's not about earning or striving but about being available and receptive to God's purposes. Embracing tongues as a spiritual discipline can facilitate a deeper experience with the gifts of the Spirit, enabling believers to serve the body of Christ with power and precision.

Let us remain eager and open to the Holy Spirit's workings, allowing Him to equip us with gifts that further His kingdom and glorify His name.

Day 10- Word of Wisdom

The Word of Wisdom is a supernatural gift of the Spirit, granting insight into God's will and purpose for specific situations. It transcends human intellect, providing guidance and solutions to perplexing problems that seem beyond resolution. This gift often serves to navigate complex circumstances with clarity and precision.

When Solomon prayed for wisdom, God granted him insight that astonished the world. Similarly, the Word of Wisdom enables believers to address challenges with God's perspective. It might manifest in a sudden understanding during prayer, a strategic idea to overcome an obstacle, or timely advice that transforms a difficult situation.

To operate effectively in this gift, we must remain humble, dependent on God,

Walking in Power

and sensitive to the Spirit's promptings. Through the Word of Wisdom, God demonstrates His care and sovereignty, equipping His people to act as agents of His purpose in the world. Let us seek and value this precious gift, trusting that when God speaks, His wisdom is perfect and His timing is always right.

"If any of you lacks wisdom, let him ask of God, who gives to all liberally and without reproach, and it will be given to him." ~ James 1:5

God is generous and willing to give wisdom to anyone who sincerely seeks it, without criticism or hesitation. Remember, we all need wisdom that is God-inspired because thinking we know it all leads to error. Let us desire to operate in the gifts that the Lord sees fit for us.

Day 11- Word of Knowledge

"For the Spirit searches everything, even the depths of God." ~1 Corinthians 2:10

The Word of Knowledge is a supernatural gift of the Spirit, granting insight into God's divine mind and plans. It reveals hidden truths or facts that cannot be discovered through natural means, enabling believers to know things that only God could reveal.

This gift often operates to edify and encourage others or to bring clarity to a situation. For example, Jesus demonstrated the Word of Knowledge when He revealed the Samaritan woman's life circumstances at the well (John 4:16-19). His words pierced through her defenses, leading her to recognize Him as the Messiah.

Walking in Power

The Word of Knowledge is not about human intellect or logic; it is a direct download from God, given to accomplish His purposes. Whether it's revealing the need for prayer, uncovering hidden sin, or providing comfort and assurance, this gift reminds us of God's intimate involvement in our lives.

To operate in the Word of Knowledge, we must cultivate a life of prayer, attentiveness to the Holy Spirit, and trust in God's wisdom. When this gift is used faithfully, it brings glory to God, strengthens the faith of His people, and advances His kingdom.

Let us stay open to the Spirit, trusting Him to reveal what we need to know at the right time. In every instance, the Word of Knowledge is a testament to God's omniscience and His deep care for His creation.

Day 12- Discerning of Spirits

"Beloved, do not believe every spirit, but test the spirits to see whether they are from God." ~1 John 4:1

1 John 4:1 warns believers to be discerning and not to accept every spiritual influence without question. It encourages testing the spirits, or the messages and teachings we encounter, to ensure they align with God's truth. Not all spiritual influences come from God, so it's important to evaluate them based on Scripture and the guidance of the Holy Spirit.

The gift of Discerning of Spirits is a powerful tool given by the Holy Spirit to reveal the true nature of spiritual activity. This gift protects believers from deception, helping them navigate spiritual matters with wisdom and truth. For example, the Apostle Paul exercised this gift when he discerned the spirit of divination operating through a slave girl (Acts 16:16-18). While her words appeared to glorify God, Paul identified the demonic source behind her declarations and cast it out, freeing her from bondage.

Discerning of Spirits equips us to recognize the subtle tactics of the enemy, differentiate between God's voice and other influences, and affirm the authenticity of spiritual manifestations. It's a safeguard for the Church, ensuring that what we embrace aligns with God's truth.

To sharpen this gift, we must saturate our minds with Scripture, stay sensitive to the Holy Spirit, and remain committed to prayer. By relying on the Spirit's guidance, we can walk in spiritual clarity, free from confusion or fear.

The gift of discerning of spirits is not about suspicion or judgment but about revelation and protection. It allows us to see beyond the surface, aligning us with God's will and shielding His people.

Day 13- Prophecy

"But the one who prophesies speaks to people for their strengthening, encouraging, and comfort."
~1 Corinthians 14:3

Prophecy is a spiritual gift that enables believers to speak the heart and mind of God. It does not derive from human reasoning, but is a supernatural utterance that builds up, encourages, consoles, and, when necessary, warns the body of Christ.

Throughout Scripture, prophecy has served as a means to guide God's people. The prophets of the Old Testament shared divine revelations, while the New Testament believers were encouraged to earnestly desire this gift (1 Corinthians 14:1). Prophecy edifies the Church, affirming God's presence and His intimate care for His people.

Walking in Power

When utilized properly, prophecy strengthens faith, provides direction, and brings comfort during challenging times. It reminds us that God is actively involved in our lives, speaking to us in ways that resonate with our hearts and circumstances. However, prophecy must always align with Scripture, as God's Word is the ultimate standard of truth.

Prophecy is a gift to be cherished and handled with humility. Those who operate in this gift must seek God's guidance and remain sensitive to the Holy Spirit, ensuring that their words reflect His will and not their own opinions.

As we seek to grow in this gift, let us remember that the ultimate purpose of prophecy is to point people to Jesus, and strengthen His Church. It's an invitation to partner with Him in sharing His love, truth, and encouragement with the world.

Day 14- Divers Kinds of Tongues

"To another, divers kinds of tongues; to another, the interpretation of tongues."
~1 Corinthians 12:10

The term *divers* means many, highlighting the gift of speaking in various languages through the supernatural empowerment of the Holy Spirit. This gift is often first experienced during the initial baptism of the Holy Spirit, as seen in Acts 2:4, where the disciples began speaking in different tongues, declaring the wonders of God in languages they had never learned.

This gift serves as a powerful sign of God's presence and purpose. It allows believers to communicate divine truths in ways that go beyond human limitations. In a corporate setting, divers kinds of tongues, when paired with interpretation, edify and strengthen the Church. In personal prayer, it enables believers to commune deeply with God, praying mysteries directly from their spirit (1 Corinthians 14:2).

The ability to speak in several languages through the Holy Spirit is a reminder of the inclusive nature of God's kingdom. It reflects His desire for the Gospel to reach all nations, breaking through cultural and linguistic barriers to bring salvation and unity to His people.

This gift invites believers to embrace the fullness of the Spirit's work, to be vessels of His power, and to participate in His global mission with courage and faith.

Day 15- Interpretation of Tongues

"To another the interpretation of tongues." ~1 Corinthians 12:10

The gift of the Interpretation of Tongues is a supernatural ability given by the Holy Spirit to understand and communicate what is spoken in unknown languages. This gift bridges the gap between a message delivered in tongues and the understanding of the hearers, ensuring that the Church is edified and God's will is revealed clearly.

Unlike translation, which relies on human knowledge of languages, interpretation is entirely Spirit-led. It enables the one interpreting to convey the essence and meaning of a message spoken in an unknown tongue. This gift often works alongside the Gift of Tongues in a corporate setting, turning what may seem mysterious into an opportunity for encouragement, instruction, and worship.

The Apostle Paul emphasized the importance of this gift, particularly in public worship, so that the congregation can understand and benefit from what is being communicated (1 Corinthians 14:13). Through the Interpretation of Tongues, God reveals His heart and purposes, inspiring unity, faith, and reverence among His people.

This gift reminds believers of the order and clarity that the Holy Spirit brings, showcasing God's desire for all to know and experience His truth. It is a beautiful demonstration of His commitment to ensuring His Word is accessible, impactful, and transformative in the lives of His people.

Day 16- Gift of Faith

"But without faith it is impossible to please him: for he that cometh to God must believe that he is, and that he is a rewarder of them that diligently seek him." ~Hebrews 11:6

The Gift of Faith is a supernatural endowment from the Holy Spirit, enabling believers to trust God beyond the limits of human doubt, logic, or reasoning. This divine faith allows us to see the unseen and believe for the impossible, anchored not in circumstances but in the unchanging character and promises of God.

This gift is not ordinary faith for salvation but a heightened level of trust that enables believers to stand firm in the face of overwhelming challenges. It empowers them to declare and expect miraculous outcomes, even when human understanding says otherwise.

Throughout Scripture, we see examples of this extraordinary faith at work—Abraham trusting God to make him the father of nations, even in his old age; Daniel remaining steadfast in the lion's den; and Peter walking on water at Jesus' command. These acts of faith defied human reasoning and glorified God by demonstrating His power.

The Gift of Faith is essential for advancing the Kingdom of God. It strengthens us to act boldly, intercede powerfully, and endure confidently. When we operate in this gift, we become vessels through which God performs extraordinary works, inspiring others to trust Him deeply.

Faith, as a supernatural gift, reminds us that nothing is impossible for God. It urges us to step out in boldness, knowing that He is faithful to fulfill His promises and accomplish His purposes through us.

Nichol Collins

Day 17- Gift of Healing

"And these signs shall follow them that believe; In my name shall they cast out devils; they shall speak with new tongues; they shall take up serpents; and if they drink any deadly thing, it shall not hurt them; they shall lay hands on the sick, and they shall recover."
~Mark 16:17-18

The Gift of Healing is a supernatural ability given by the Holy Spirit to restore individuals to physical, emotional, and spiritual wholeness, beyond the limits of natural healing. It is God's divine power working through believers to bring about miraculous cures for all kinds of sickness, disease, and affliction—without the use of human medicine or effort.

In the Gospels, Jesus demonstrated the gift of healing time and again. He healed the blind, the lame, the lepers, and even raised the dead. The apostles continued this work after His ascension, laying hands on the sick and seeing them recover. These healings weren't just acts of kindness; they were signs pointing to the Kingdom of God breaking through into the world.

When we walk in the Gift of Healing, we are joining in that same mission to bring heaven's restoration to earth. We are not merely asking God to heal; we are participating in His redemptive work, extending His love and power to others. When we see healing happen—whether it's instant or over time—it builds our faith and reminds us of the deep love God has for His creation. Just as Jesus healed the multitudes, we are called to be vessels of His healing power in the world today, showing the world that the Kingdom of God has come near.

Day 18- Working of Miracles

"Jesus looked at them and said, 'With man this is impossible, but with God all things are possible.'" ~Matthew 19:26

The Working of Miracles is a gift that enables believers to become conduits for God's miraculous power. When the Holy Spirit empowers us with this gift, we become instruments in God's hands, capable of impacting lives in extraordinary ways. A miracle might be physical—healing a disease or performing a dramatic act of provision. It could also be spiritual, breaking strongholds or bringing restoration to broken lives. Regardless of the nature of the miracle, it always points to God's glory, showing the world that He is active, powerful, and ever-present.

In Scripture, we see Jesus performing countless miracles—turning water into

Walking in Power

wine, feeding thousands with a small amount of food, walking on water, calming storms, and raising the dead. These miracles were not simply demonstrations of power; they were signs of God's Kingdom breaking into the world. Through these acts, Jesus showed that God's reign is not limited by the natural world. What seems impossible to us is entirely possible with God.

As believers, we are called to have faith in the God of miracles. We are to trust that He is able to intervene in any circumstance, whether in our own lives or in the lives of others. Through the Working of Miracles, we become living testimonies of God's transformative power. When we encounter the miraculous, we are reminded that we serve a God who is not bound by time, space, or nature, but who has the power to change any situation for His glory.

Day 19- Moving Forward

The Apostle Paul captured this mindset when he declared:
"Brothers and sisters, I do not consider myself yet to have taken hold of it. But one thing I do: Forgetting what is behind and straining toward what is ahead."
~Philippians 3:13 (NIV)

In this verse, Paul acknowledges that he has not yet fully attained the ultimate goal of knowing Christ and reaching spiritual maturity. However, he emphasizes one key principle: forgetting what is behind. It is a call to live with an unwavering focus on the future God has for us, continuously striving toward spiritual growth, transformation, and the fulfillment of God's purpose in our lives.

Praying in tongues has the unique power to transition your focus from the past into the future. It aligns your spirit with God's purposes, enabling you to release what has been and embrace what lies ahead — silencing the distractions of past failures or successes. It propels you into God's future for you, helping you to focus on His promises and plans.

By letting go of the weights of yesterday and reaching toward the mark of His high calling, you are equipped to walk boldly into the fullness of what God has prepared. Tongues serve as a spiritual bridge, transitioning you from reflection to expectation, and from limitation to transformation.

Day 20- Unstoppable Progress

"For the Lord of hosts has decided and planned, and who can annul it? His hand is stretched out, and who can turn it back?" ~Isaiah 14:27 (AMP)

This verse reveals God's sovereignty—when He makes a decision, no one can stop it. His plans are unstoppable, and His power is unmatched. This verse reminds us that God's will will always prevail.

Speaking in tongues equips you with momentum, granting unstoppable progress that no opposition can overturn. It aligns your spirit with God's will, fortifying your path with the authority and power of His plan. When you engage in tongues, you partner with the Lord's unshakable decree over your life. No force—spiritual or physical—can derail the progress He has destined for you.

Walking in Power

What God has set in motion through your prayers cannot be revoked, and His hand extended in your favor cannot be hindered.

Tongues empower you to walk with confidence, knowing that your steps are ordered by a God whose plans are final and whose will is unstoppable. Let this truth encourage you to press forward in confidence, trusting that every obstacle will bow to the sovereign purpose of the Lord.

Day 21- A Love Language

As the Bride of Christ, speaking in tongues is a divine expression of love and adoration to our Beloved King. It is a sacred language of intimacy, spoken from our spirit to the heart of God. Through this heavenly dialogue, we strengthen our bond with the Lord and position ourselves in His will.

John 14:26 reminds us of the Holy Spirit's role in our lives:
"But the Comforter, which is the Holy Ghost, whom the Father will send in my name, he shall teach you all things, and bring all things to your remembrance, whatsoever I have said unto you."

The Holy Spirit equips us to express what words cannot, guiding us into a fuller understanding of God's truth and love. In tongues, we experience a profound connection with the Father, expressing adoration and worship that transcends earthly language. This unique love language strengthens our bond with the Lord, drawing us closer to Him in both spirit and truth.

As you engage in tongues, let it serve as a reminder of the intimate relationship you share with your Savior—a relationship built on love, trust, and divine communion.

Day 22- All Things Good

Romans 8:28 offers a powerful promise for those who love God and are called according to His purpose:
"And we know that all things work together for good to them that love God, to them who are the called according to his purpose."

This verse reminds us that no matter what circumstances we face, God is orchestrating every detail for our ultimate good. Challenges, trials, and even setbacks are not random; they are tools in the hands of a sovereign God who uses them to shape us, refine our character, and draw us closer to Him.

Loving God and walking in His purpose doesn't guarantee a life without difficulties, but it does guarantee that everything will have meaning and purpose. When we trust in this promise,

Walking in Power

we can face life's uncertainties with confidence, knowing that God is in control.

Be encouraged today, knowing that the outcome will always reflect what is good!

Nichol Collins

Day 23- Embracing the Mindset of Christ

"Let this mind be in you, which was also in Christ Jesus." ~Philippians 2:5

Philippians 2:5 encourages believers to adopt the mindset of Christ, embodying humility, selflessness, and a servant's heart. It calls for a shift in our attitudes and behaviors to reflect the character of Jesus—prioritizing others above ourselves and following His example of obedience to God.

Praying in tongues has a transformative effect on our thoughts and mindset. As we engage in this Spirit-led prayer, our minds become more aligned with the will and perspective of Christ. It is a divine process that transcends human understanding, allowing us to access the thoughts of God and renew our own. The mind of Christ is marked by humility, obedience, love, and a clear purpose aligned with the Father's will.

Through praying in tongues, we shift from our natural, limited way of thinking to a heavenly perspective.

This transformation helps us to discern spiritual truths, walk in wisdom, and respond to life's challenges with the grace and character of Christ. Let tongues become a tool to shape your thoughts and bring them into agreement with God's perfect plan, empowering you to live out His purpose with clarity and conviction.

Day 24- Pray Without Ceasing

"Rejoice always, pray without ceasing, give thanks in all circumstances; for this is the will of God in Christ Jesus for you."
~1 Thessalonians 5:16-18

The Apostle Paul, in his letter to the Thessalonians, calls us to a lifestyle of unceasing prayer. This isn't about being on our knees 24/7, but about cultivating an attitude of continuous connection with God throughout the day.

Praying without ceasing means staying in constant communication with our Heavenly Father, acknowledging His presence in all moments of our lives. It's not just about asking for things or requesting blessings, but about having an ongoing conversation with God—one where we express our gratitude, seek His guidance, share our concerns, and simply enjoy His presence.

Walking in Power

Paul also adds a crucial reminder: **"Give thanks in all circumstances."** Even in hardship, we can find reasons to praise God, for His love and faithfulness never fail. Our attitude of gratitude, nurtured by constant prayer, helps us to see beyond our immediate challenges and recognize God's hand in everything.

The invitation to pray without ceasing is not a burdensome demand, but a beautiful opportunity to live in constant communion with our Creator. It's about letting God be part of every aspect of our lives, allowing Him to guide, comfort, and empower us at all times. When we embrace this lifestyle, we will begin to experience His peace that surpasses all understanding, and His presence will transform every moment.

Let today be a reminder that prayer is not confined to specific moments but is a way of living in constant connection with the One who loves us deeply and desires to walk with us in every step.

Day 25- Intentional Prayer Time

"But Jesus often withdrew to lonely places and prayed." ~Luke 5:16

This verse shows Jesus' example of regularly stepping away from the demands of His ministry and the crowds to spend time alone with His Father in prayer. It pinpoints the value of quiet, intentional moments to seek guidance, renew strength, and stay connected to God—a practice Jesus, fully God and fully man, demonstrates for all believers to follow to experience the guidance and renewal that only Jesus can provide.

Prayer is not just a ritual or a rushed routine—it is a sacred time set aside to engage with God. In our busy lives, it's easy to forget that prayer is meant to be a personal and intimate connection with our Creator. While it's true that we can pray "on the go" throughout the day— while driving, working, or caring for others—it's crucial that we don't fall into the habit of neglecting quality time with the Lord.

Our prayer time should never be just a task to check off a to-do list. Instead, it should be purposeful and focused. Just as we carve out time for meals, work, and rest, we must also prioritize setting aside time for prayer. This time is for us to hear from God, to reflect on His Word, and to build our relationship with Him.

Think of your day like slices of a pie representing different responsibilities. While work, family, and personal time are important, we must first reserve a slice for God. It's about finding balance—ensuring that our spiritual needs are met alongside our other obligations.

In a world that often feels chaotic and full of distractions, taking time to slow down and pray is essential. It's in these moments that we can hear God's voice more clearly, receive His wisdom, and be filled with His peace. Psalm 46:10, "Be still, and know that I am God," reminds us to quiet our minds, surrender control, and trust that God is in control of all things.

Day 26- Watch Him Work

"Commit your way to the Lord; trust in Him, and He will act." ~Psalm 37:5

In a world where we are constantly making decisions, planning our futures, and navigating uncertainties, Psalm 37:5 offers us a profound and reassuring promise. To **commit our way** means to dedicate every part of our life, from the smallest daily tasks to the grandest dreams, to God's will. It is an invitation to stop relying solely on our own understanding and control and instead entrust our path to God's wisdom and direction.

Trusting in Him follows closely behind commitment. Trust is more than just a word; it's an action. It is the belief that God knows what is best for us and that His plans are higher than ours (Isaiah 55:9). Trusting in the Lord means we release our anxieties about what lies ahead, knowing that God will lead us in the right direction, even if the journey isn't always clear or easy.

And here's the beautiful promise: **He will act.** When we commit our way to the Lord and trust Him, He will not leave us to navigate life on our own. God will **act**—He will move on our behalf, He will guide our steps, and He will bring about His perfect will in our lives. Even in times of uncertainty, we can rest assured that God is at work, orchestrating everything for our good (Romans 8:28).

So, today, take a moment to reflect on the areas of your life that you may be holding on to tightly. What are you trying to control, and where do you need to release your grip? Commit those areas to the Lord and trust in His ability to act on your behalf. He is faithful, and His plans for you are good.

Day 27- The Lord's Abundance

"The Lord will open to you His good treasury, the heavens, to give the rain to your land in its season and to bless all the work of your hands."
~Deuteronomy 28:12

This verse reveals God's promise of abundant provision. Like rain that nourishes the land, God ensures that we prosper. When we commit our work to Him, it becomes an avenue of His timely favor. Whether we're in need financially, spiritually, or emotionally — God's blessings lead to a life of abundance, and enables us to be a blessing to those around us.

Trust God for His provision in your life, knowing that He will bless you at the right time and in every area of your life. As He blesses you, remember to give to the less fortunate and pray about investments. Stewardship is vital!

Day 28- Led by the Spirit

"For as many as are led by the Spirit of God, they are the sons of God."
~Romans 8:14

This powerful verse speaks of the intimate relationship between God and His children. Those who are led by the Holy Spirit are identified as God's sons and daughters. It's a call to live under the guidance and influence of the Spirit, recognizing that our identity as children of God is rooted in following His lead.

The Holy Spirit is not just a comforter but also a guide. He directs our decisions, helps us make wise choices, and reveals God's will for our lives. When we follow His guidance, we align ourselves with the Father's purpose for us.

Being led by the Spirit is a mark of sonship. It's not about our human efforts,

Walking in Power

but about surrendering to God's plan and living in obedience to His leading. As His children, we have the privilege of living in His will, empowered by His Spirit.

Are you allowing the Holy Spirit to lead you? Take time today to listen for His guidance in your life. Embrace the peace that comes from knowing that as you follow Him, you are walking in your true identity as a child of God.

Day 29- Knowing the Scriptures

"Jesus replied, 'Your mistake is that you don't know the Scriptures, and you don't know the power of God.'"
~Matthew 22:29

In this verse, Jesus addresses a group of people who were misguided because they lacked understanding in two key areas: the Scriptures and the power of God. Jesus makes it clear that both are essential for a deeper relationship with Him and for living out His will.

The Scriptures are not just historical accounts or moral teachings; they are the living Word of God. When we truly know and understand the Word, it transforms our hearts and minds. It's through the Scriptures that we learn who God is, His promises to us, and how we should live in response to His love.

Walking in Power

Jesus also emphasizes the importance of knowing the power of God. It's not enough to simply know about God; we must experience His power in our lives. The same power that raised Jesus from the dead is available to us today to bring healing, deliverance, and transformation.

Do you know the Scriptures? Are you experiencing the power of God in your daily life? Take time today to immerse yourself in the Word, seeking both understanding and the active presence of God's power in your life. As you grow in both areas, you'll find yourself walking in greater authority and victory.

Day 30- A Living Well

*"But whosoever drinketh of the water that I shall give him shall never thirst; but the water that I shall give him shall be in him a well of water springing up into everlasting life." ~*John 4:14

In this passage, Jesus offers us a profound promise—the living water that satisfies our deepest thirst. This water is not just physical; it represents the spiritual life that only He can give. When we receive the Holy Spirit, we are filled with this living water, a continual wellspring that flows from within, enabling us to live in victory and communion with God.

The power of tongues is a direct connection to this living water. As we pray in the Spirit, we tap into the endless source of God's strength, wisdom, and peace. Just as a well continually

Walking in Power

provides fresh water, our prayer language continually connects us to God's presence, bringing nourishment to our spirit. It is in this deep communion with the Holy Spirit that we are refreshed, renewed, and strengthened.

This living water is not something we can obtain apart from Jesus. He is the source, and it is only through our relationship with Him that we experience the fullness of His power in our lives. The more we seek Him, the more His Spirit flows through us. The key is regular communion—spending time in prayer, worship, and Scripture, allowing the water of life to flow freely and continually within us.

Are you staying connected to the Source of living water? Are you allowing the Holy Spirit to flow through you, refreshing and empowering you? Make time today to drink deeply from the well of God's presence, knowing that as you do, you will never thirst again.

A Simple Guide to Receive the Holy Spirit

If you're ready to experience the Holy Spirit, know that He is knocking at the door of your heart, waiting for you to invite Him in. Jesus offers the gift of the Holy Spirit freely to those who ask (Luke 11:13). This gift is not about eloquent words but a heart that is open and willing.Jesus loves you and wants to empower you with His Spirit. Relax and trust Him.

Step 1: Ask for Forgiveness
Begin by asking Jesus to forgive you of your sins. The prayer doesn't have to be perfect; God is looking at your heart.

Step 2: Praise with Expectancy
Say, "Thank you, Jesus," repeatedly, with gratitude and expectancy for the gift of the Holy Spirit. This praise should come from your heart, not as a repetitive chant, but with anticipation for what God

is about to do. You are praising with gratitude.

Step 3: Yield to the Holy Spirit
As you praise, you may begin to feel a shift in your speech. Your words may seem jumbled or like baby talk—don't be afraid. These are the early signs of the Holy Spirit moving within you. Trust God, speak out the unknown sounds.

Step 4: Speak in Faith
Do not worry about what it sounds like. The Holy Spirit is giving you the ability to speak in a heavenly language (1 Cor. 14:2). Keep trusting Him, and allow the Spirit to flow from your belly.

Step 5: Keep Going
The more you speak, the clearer the language will become. Don't worry about how it sounds or whether you understand it—this is a gift from God.

Keep speaking in tongues as He gives you the words. This is your new heavenly language!

www.ingramcontent.com/pod-product-compliance
Lightning Source LLC
Chambersburg PA
CBHW052222090426
42741CB00010B/2641